Easy Jazz HANON

50 Exercises for the Beginning to Professional Pianist

by Peter Deneff

Now including **PLAYBACK+**, *a multi-functional audio player that allows you to slow down audio without changing pitch, set loop points, change keys, and pan left or right—available exclusively from Hal Leonard.*

PLAYBACK+
Speed • Pitch • Balance • Loop

To access audio visit:
www.halleonard.com/mylibrary

Enter Code
3116-8598-8706-3265

ISBN 978-1-4950-8229-0

7777 W. BLUEMOUND RD. P.O. BOX 13819 MILWAUKEE, WI 53213

In Australia Contact:
Hal Leonard Australia Pty. Ltd.
4 Lentara Court
Cheltenham, Victoria, 3192 Australia
Email: ausadmin@halleonard.com.au

Visit Hal Leonard Online at
www.halleonard.com

Acknowledgements

I would like to thank all the people in my life who have encouraged and supported me in my musical journey. My parents, George V. Deneff and Alkisti Deneff, my children, Gitana, George, and Sophia, and most of all, my wife, Diane, who continues to inspire, encourage and support me in my life and career. Lastly, I would like to thank all of the musicians and fans who continue to support me through my performances, recordings, and of course, enjoying my books!

About the author

Peter Deneff grew up in a musical home, exposed to classical music, Greek songs, and the Beatles. After several years of classical piano lessons with Leaine Gibson, he began jazz studies with the world-renowned pianist and David Bowie band member, Mike Garson. During this time he also studied many ethnic styles that influenced his composition and playing. He studied music composition and film scoring at California State University Long Beach, where he earned his bachelor's and master's degrees in classical music composition. While at CSULB, Deneff composed his *Three Greek Dances for String Quartet*, which has been performed in the U.S., Canada, and Australia.

Peter has written many best-selling books for Hal Leonard Corporation and has produced and recorded numerous arrangements for Yamaha, Hal Leonard, and PianoDisc. His original music and scoring was featured in the award-winning Charlie Sheen film, *Five Aces*. In 2012, Deneff composed the score for the feature film *Love of Life*. In early 2013, his involvement with the Hollywood animation community afforded him the opportunity to write the score for the short film, "The Annies: 40 Year Retrospective" which was presented as one of the highlights of the 2013 Annie Awards at Royce Hall, UCLA, and featured the legendary voice actress June Foray. Also, in 2013, Deneff scored the film, *A Journey into the Holocaust*, produced by Paul Bachow.

His stylistic versatility on the keyboard has allowed him to perform with a diverse assortment of artists such as Tierra, Ike Willis (Frank Zappa), Ramon Banda, Jerry Salas (El Chicano), Chalo Eduardo as well as jazz greats, Robert Kyle, Bruce Babad, Bijon Watson, and Tom Brechtlein. Deneff has also performed and directed numerous international recording artists like Sonia Santos, Rita Sakellariou, Giorgos Margaritis, Stathis Aggelopoulos, Vatche, Shimi Tavori, and Persian international superstar Ebi.

Deneff's original project, Excursion, features mostly original works in a style that could be best described as *ethno-jazz*. Excursion's sound is a blend of Brazilian, Cuban, Greek, Armenian, classical, and progressive jazz. The group has been featured twice at the Playboy Jazz Festival and regularly performs at Herb Alpert's Vibrato Jazz Grill and at the World Famous Baked Potato in Hollywood.

On the academic side, Peter has taught at Musician's Institute Hollywood, Orange County High School of the Arts, Cypress College, and currently enjoys teaching at Fullerton College in California.

Introduction

The study of jazz piano can be a daunting task for any musician, but it can be an even bigger challenge for the beginning to intermediate student. In the early years of playing, many students are still struggling with note reading, difficult key signatures, and/or limited technical dexterity. This is where *Easy Jazz Hanon* comes in. This book was written especially for the aforementioned students. Whereas the original *Jazz Hanon* was written with the more advanced player in mind, this book is intended to be approachable by nearly all pianists, regardless of level.

Some of the features of this volume include chord symbols, easy keys, and backing tracks, all of which can help the less-experienced student get up and running. More advanced students can tailor the exercises to make them more challenging. For instance, any exercise in the book could (and should!) be practiced in all twelve keys. All the exercises are short and non-sequential. The student can explore throughout the book and practice any of the studies they find interesting and useful. The general goal is to build technique and dexterity while learning chord voicings and jazz feel.

This collection includes both melodic and harmonic exercises. The melodic exercises feature idiomatic runs and phrases that one would actually play within a jazz context. The harmonic exercises feature typical jazz chord voicings that are essential to the style. All the studies are written in swing 8ths and some employ other typical jazz rhythms such as 16th notes and 8th note triplets. The play-along tracks provide a fun way to practice these exercises and also allow the student to hear a demo of them being played.

Here are some suggestions to help maximize your results:
- Start slowly and don't practice any exercise faster than you can accurately play it.
- Always use a metronome or the play-along tracks.
- Keep your fingers curved, hands low, and play on your fingertips.
- Observe the recommended fingerings.
- Maintain good posture, stay relaxed, and breathe!
- Memorize the exercises and internalize the patterns.
- Be creative with them, compose variations, and most importantly…have fun!

I hope that this volume will become a staple of your practice regimen. The exercises address all three elements of music: melody, harmony, and rhythm. They are accessible to all pianists, regardless of level, and are adaptable to different sub-genres of jazz, such as Latin jazz and fusion. No matter how you decide to employ these etudes, they are sure to provide an enjoyable and satisfying approach to developing your jazz chops and finger strength.

Happy practicing!

Peter Deneff

1

2

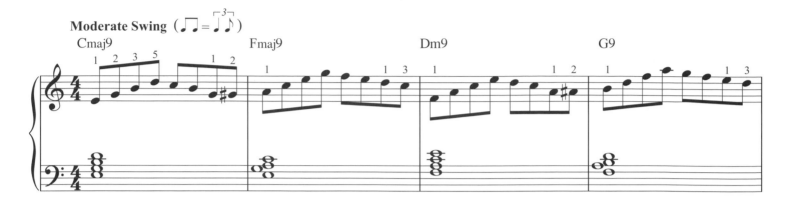

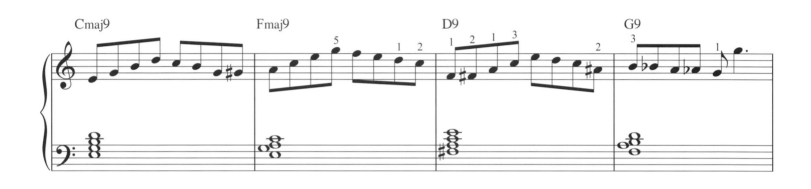

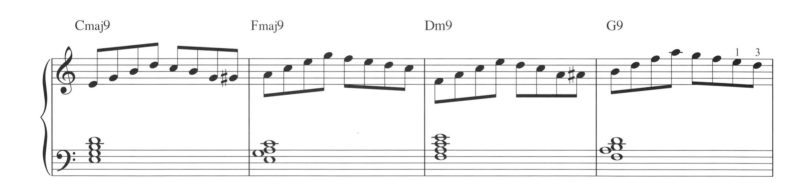

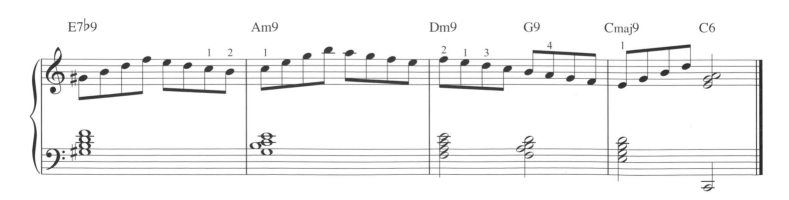

3

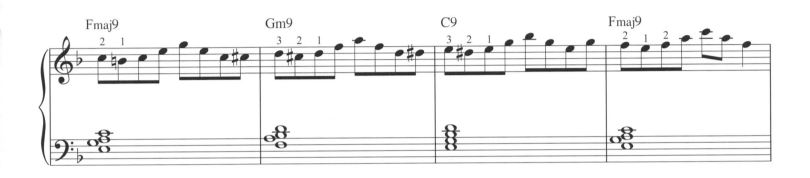

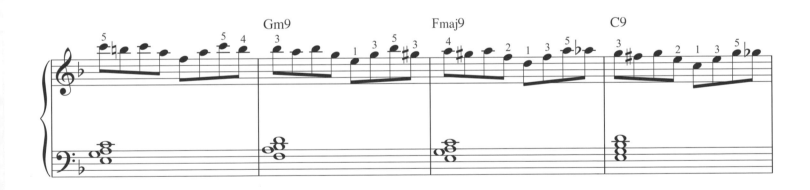

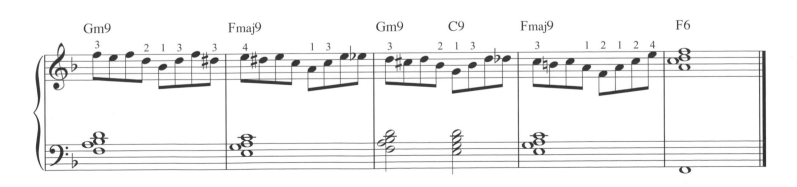

4

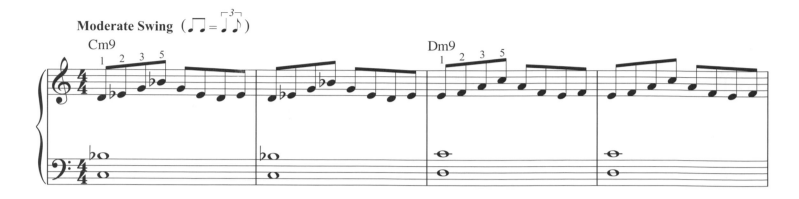

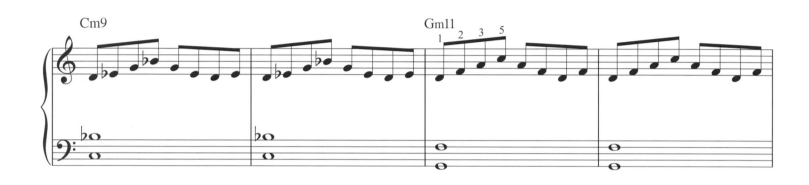

5

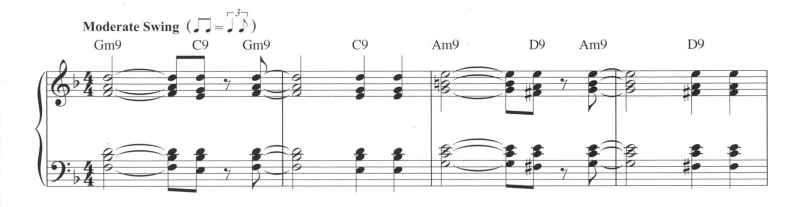

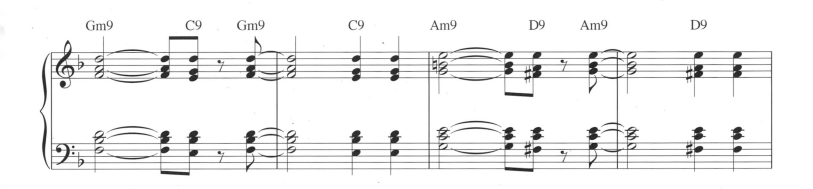

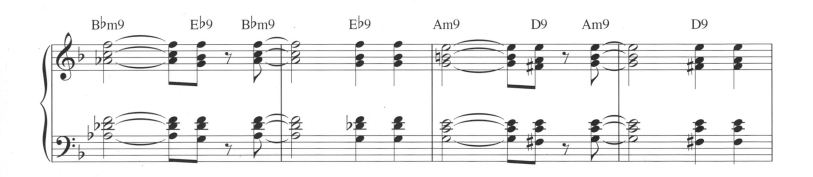

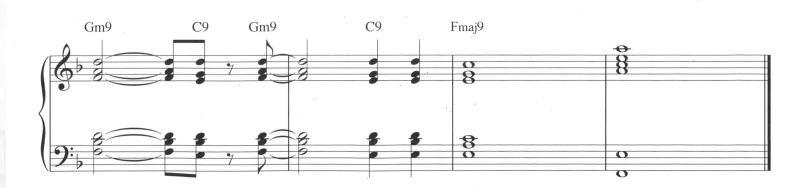

6

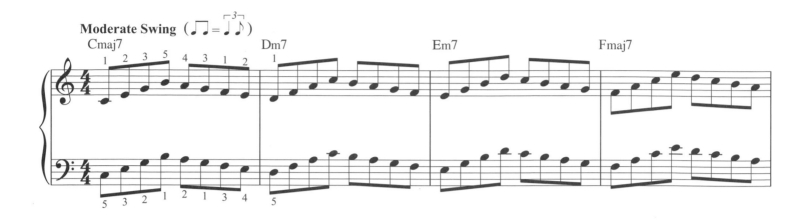

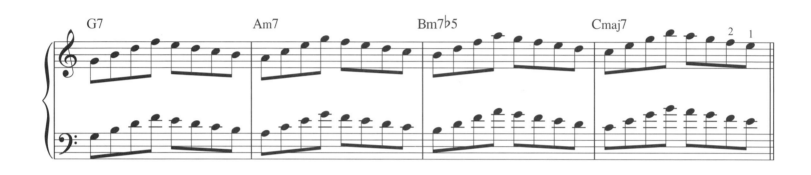

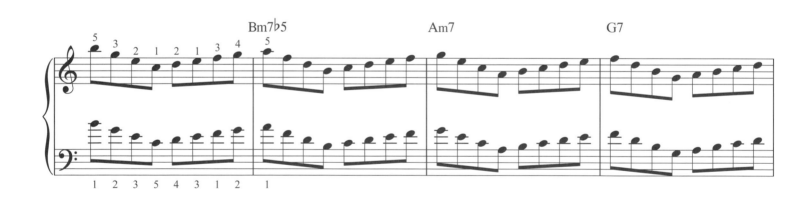

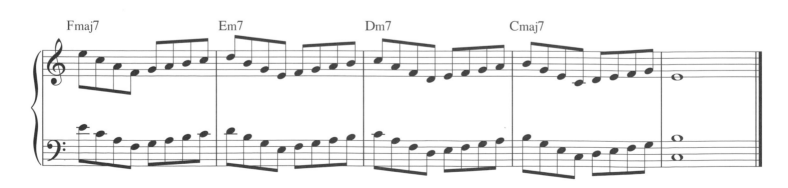

7

8

10

11

12

13

14

15

16

17

18

19

20

21

22

23

24

25

26

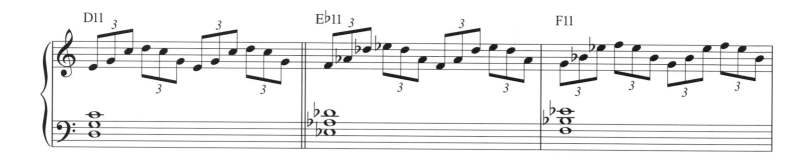

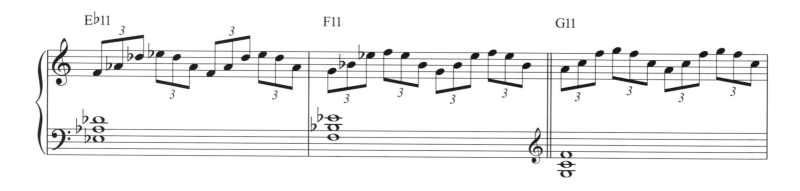

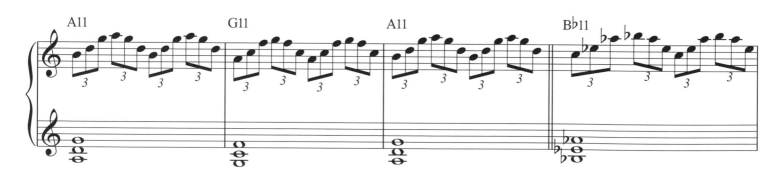

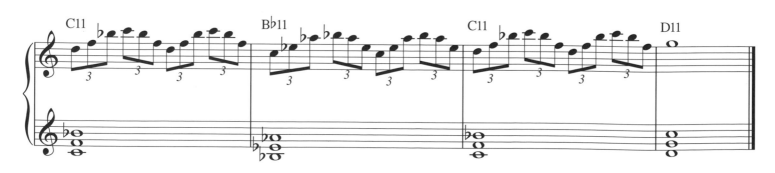

27

28

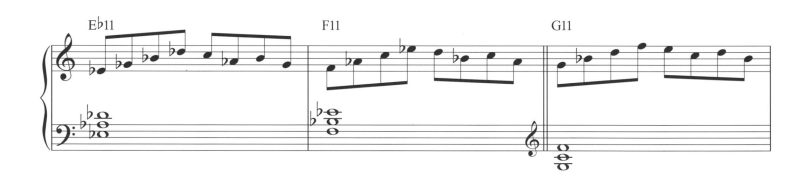

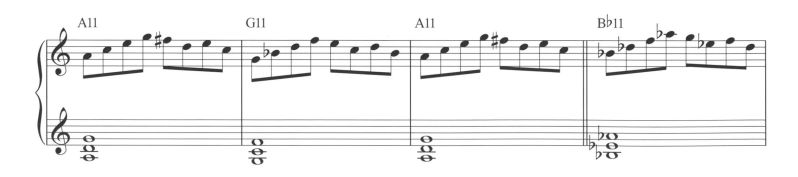

29

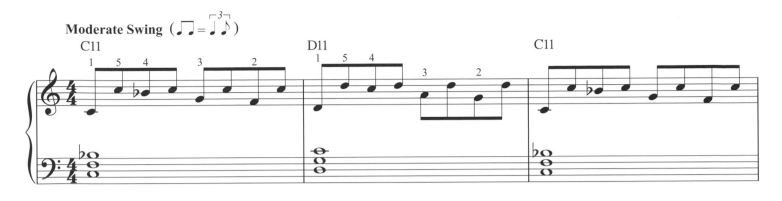

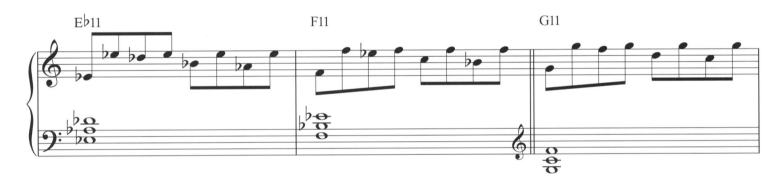

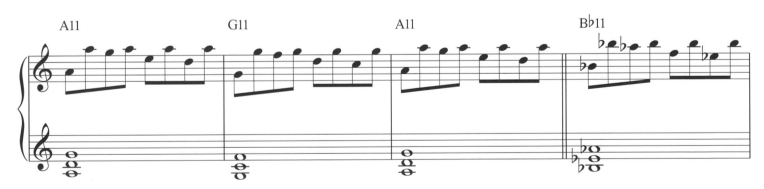

30

Moderate Swing

31

32

33

34

35

36

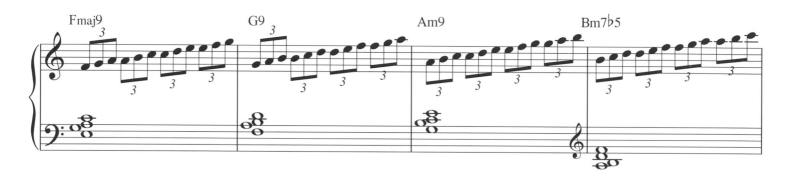

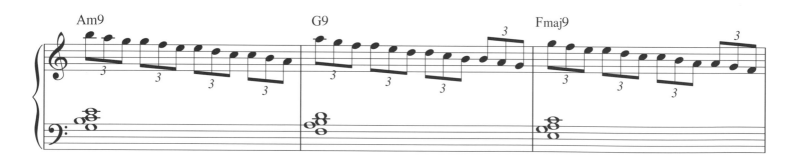

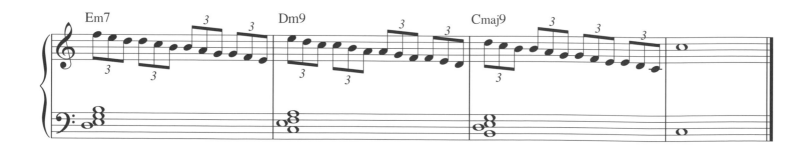

37

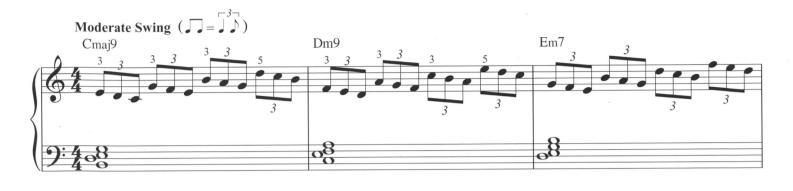

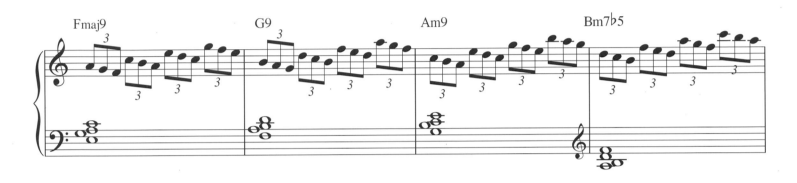

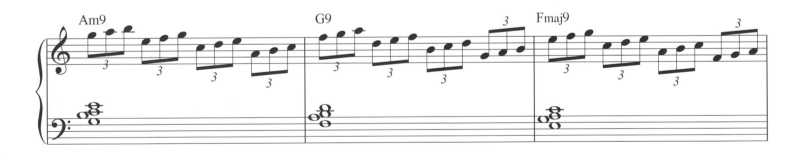

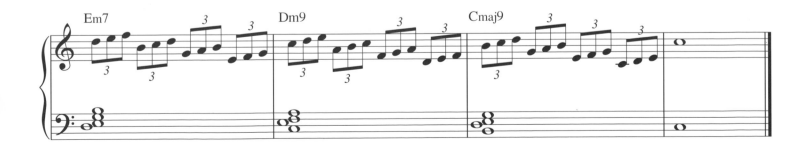

38

39

40

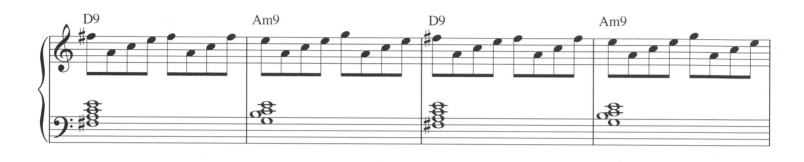

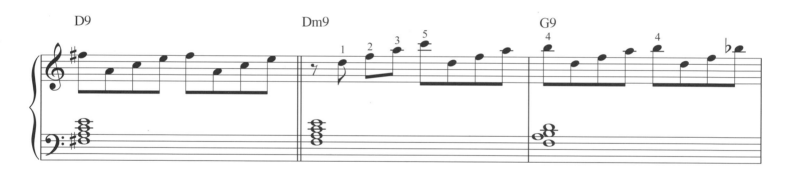

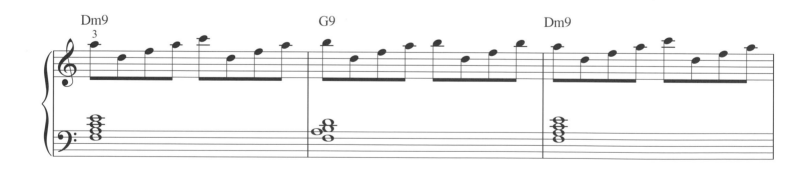

41

42

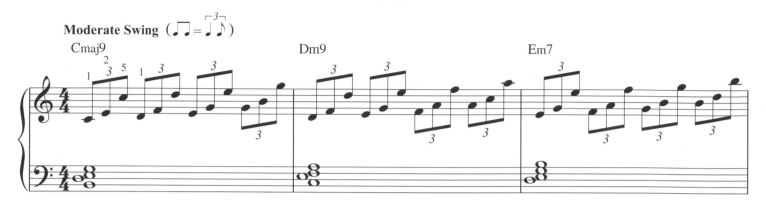

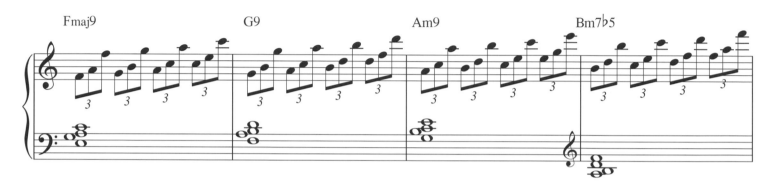

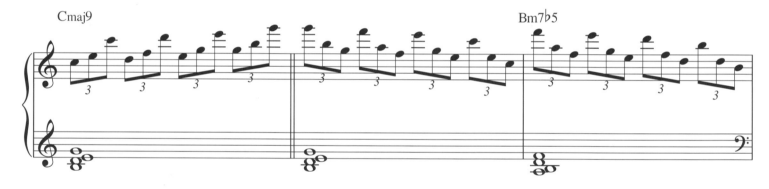

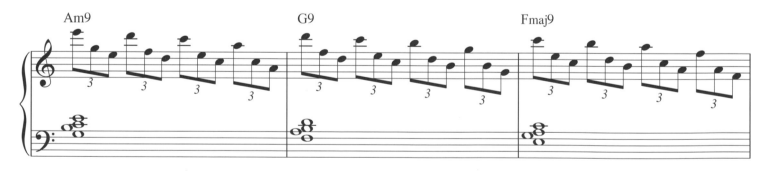

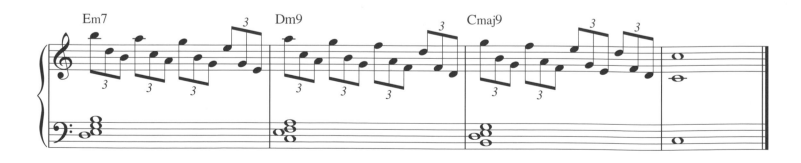

43

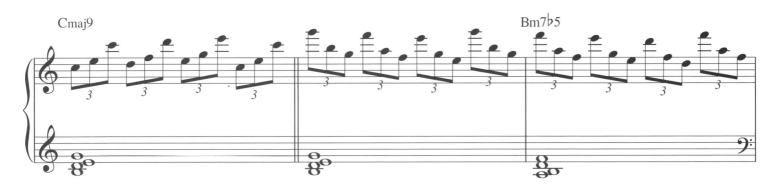

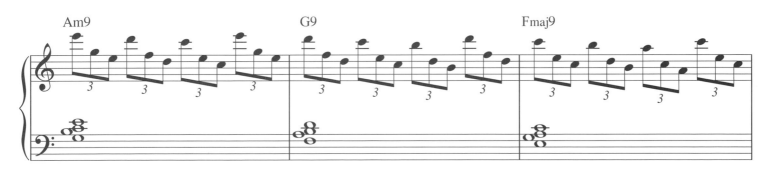

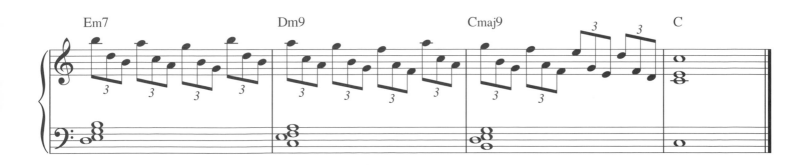

44

45

46

47

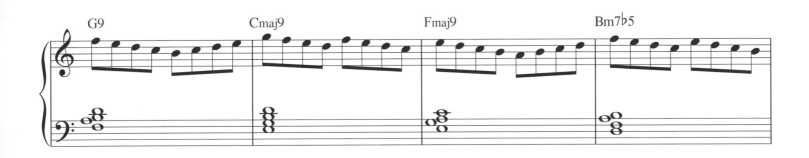

48

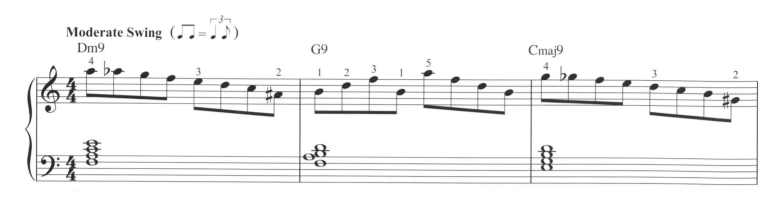

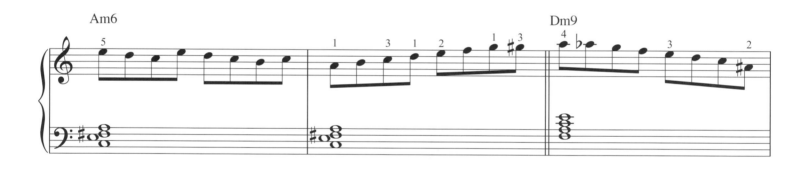

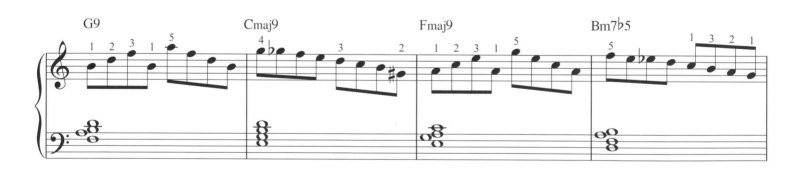

49

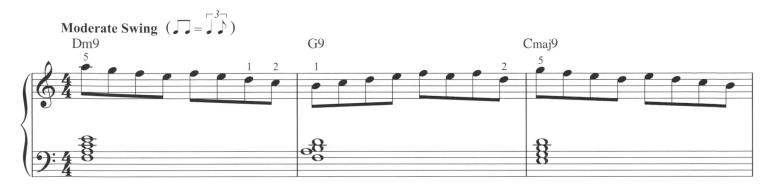

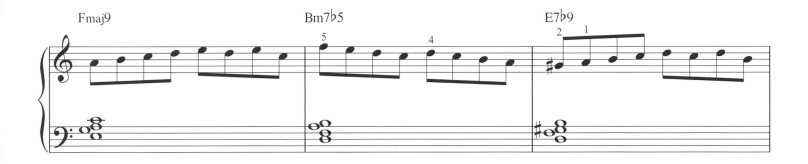

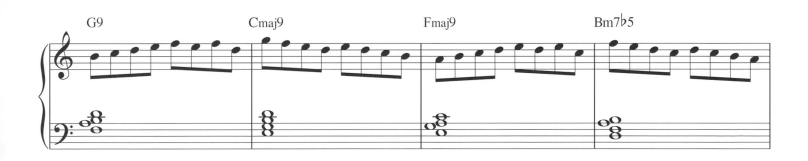

50

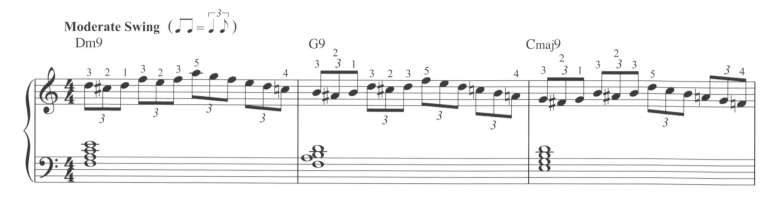

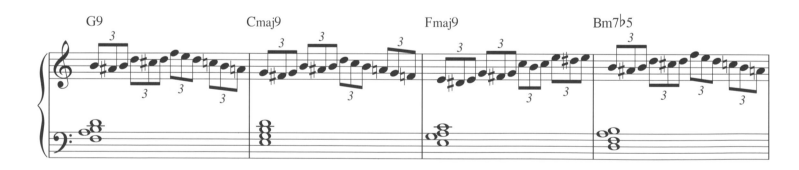

MUSICIANS INSTITUTE PRESS is the official series of instructional publications from Southern California's renowned music school. These publications have been created by MI instructors who are among the world's best and most experienced professional musicians.

Blues Hanon
by Peter Deneff
In this private lesson for beginning to professional blues pianists, Deneff covers: major and minor blues modes; workouts for the right and left hand; building fluency in all 12 keys; suggested fingerings; practice tips; and soul, gospel, boogie woogie, R&B and rock styles.

00695708 Book $16.95

Jazz Hanon
by Peter Deneff
Now available with a play-along CD! 50 exercises for the beginning to professional jazz pianist, covering: angular lines, large intervals, pentatonic patterns, blues scales, irregular chromatic melodies, double-note patterns, and more.

00696478 Book/CD Pack $19.99

Rock Hanon
by Peter Deneff
This volume for rock keyboardists features 70 essential exercises in a variety of styles: classic rock, pop, progressive rock, rockabilly and more, all based on the requisite Hanon studies.

00695784 Book $16.99

Dictionary of Keyboard Grooves
by Gail Johnson
The first comprehensive source for keyboard grooves complete with transcriptions and tips on loop construction! Covers: dance, funk, jazz, Latin, reggae, R&B and rock 'n' roll grooves.

00695556 Book/CD Pack $16.95

Jazz Piano
by Christian Klikovits
This book/CD covers all aspects of jazz piano: seventh, altered and extended chords • progressions • rootless and octave voicings • tritone substitution • functional and chromatic harmony • scales and modes • building melodies • and more.

00695773 Book/CD Pack $19.99

Salsa Hanon Play-Along
by Peter Deneff
Now available with a play-along CD! This bestselling book is intended as a sequel to Hanon's *The Virtuoso Pianist*. It is perfect for the beginning to professional pianist.

00696422 Book/CD Pack $19.99

Funk Keyboards – The Complete Method
by Gail Johnson
Subjects covered include: common chords and progressions; classic funk rhythms, licks and patterns; synth bass & multiple keyboard playing; and pitch wheel and modulation.

00695336 Book/Online Audio $16.99

Keyboard Voicings
by Kevin King
Everything keyboardists need to know about voicings, covering: triads, seventh chords, extended chords, suspended chords and altered chords; inversions; voice leading; intervals; diatonic harmony; and more!

00695209 Book $12.95

Samba Hanon
by Peter Deneff
50 essential Latin patterns for all pianists! Covers styles such as samba, bossa nova, lambada, bahia and partido alto, and artists including João Gilberto, Antonio Carlos Jobim, Astrud Gilberto, Gilberto Gil and others.

00695939 Book $16.99

Hip-Hop Keyboard
by Henry Soleh Brewer
A hands-on guide to essential hip-hop and rap keyboard techniques. Covers all keyboard instruments, sampling and loops, rhythmic feel and groove, and more.

00695936 Book/CD Pack $17.95

Pop Keyboard Concepts
by Christian Klikovits
Topics include: scale types and application • chord types and progressions • rhythmic subdivision and syncopation • improvisation concepts • comping patterns • ideas for soloing • and more.

00145419 Book/Online Audio $19.99

Stride Hanon
by Peter Deneff
50 essential exercises for the beginning to professional pianist based on the requisite Hanon studies. The exercises address: stride, ragtime, Broadway, honky-tonk, New Orleans, Harlem stride, 2-beat swing, and more.

00695882 Book $17.99

Jazz Chord Hanon
by Peter Deneff
Jazz Chord Hanon provides 70 essential exercises in a variety of styles to benefit beginning to professional jazz keyboardist, all based on the requisite Hanon studies.

00695791 Book $17.99

Pop Rock Keyboards
by Henry Sol-Eh Brewer & David Garfield
Learn the essential theory, history, various styles and techniques that every aspiring pop and rock keyboardist should know.

00695509 Book/CD Pack $19.95

HAL•LEONARD®
www.halleonard.com

0217

ALL JAZZED UP!